Kids' Guide to Making Friends

How to Build Social Skills, Handle Emotions, Speak Up, Resolve Conflicts, and Create Lasting Friendships

By

Jamie Thorne

ISBN: 978-1-962481-00-7
Copyright 2023.
Elk Point Press.

For questions,
please reach out to connect@elkpointpress.com

FREE BONUS

SCAN TO GET OUR NEXT BOOK FOR FREE!

TABLE OF CONTENTS

INTRODUCTION

If you've ever moved to a new city or changed schools, you know it can be hard to make new friends. You may have all sorts of questions. What if no one likes me? What if they laugh at me? These worries are very common, and most people experience these kinds of doubts and insecurities at some point in their lives. However, in this book you'll learn that making new friends is possible, and can even be lots of fun.

In this book, we will also talk about what to do once you've made new friends, like how to be loyal and how to grow your friendships over time. We'll discuss some tips for being a great friend, which is a skill that will serve you well throughout your life.

First, let's start with a quiz. Give yourself three points for each statement that is definitely always true for you, two points for each statement that is sometimes true for you, and one point for each statement that is hardly ever true for you.

So, the scale is: 3 = definitely true; 2 = sometimes true; 1 = hardly ever true

1. I can easily walk up to someone I don't know and start talking.
2. I think I'm pretty good at making friends.
3. I usually keep friends for a long time.
4. I always apologize when I accidentally hurt a friend's feelings.
5. I know how to handle problems with friends when they happen.
6. Lots of people seem to want to be my friend.
7. I have one person I consider to be my best friend and we get along really well.
8. My friends invite me to their homes a lot and I invite them to mine.

9. I am a good sport when I play games with my friends.
10. I stick up for a friend if they are in trouble.

Add up your points. If you scored 20 to 30 points, congrats! You have some great friendship habits already. If you scored lower or had a hard time answering the questions, don't worry. The techniques we'll discuss in this book will help you make friends and keep those friendships alive for years.

In this book, we'll discuss many topics related to friendship and how to be a good friend.

In Chapter 1, we'll discuss what a friend is, what the benefits of friendship are, and how to be a good friend.

In Chapter 2, we'll talk about how to get to know people — how to find common ground and meet new people.

In Chapter 3, we'll discuss why it's important to step back to make friends.

Chapter 4 is all about handling stressful situations, including how to use some calming strategies when you are stressed.

In Chapter 5, we'll talk about speaking up to share with friends.

Chapter 6 is all about getting through difficult situations with friends.

In Chapter 7, we'll talk about blending in to join friends, as well as how to be a good playdate and guest host.

Chapter 8 will cover some activities you can try that will help you develop social skills.

Finally, in Chapter 9, we'll talk about how to keep friendships growing as you get older.

Are you ready? Okay, let's get started....

CHAPTER ONE:
WHAT IS A FRIEND?

So, what is a friend? The dictionary describes a friend as "a person attached to another by feelings of affection or personal regard." Simply put, friends are people who you care about and who also care about you. You might not love them the way you love your family, but you trust them and feel good when you spend time with them.

THE BENEFITS
OF FRIENDSHIP

People with friends often feel like they belong and have a purpose. They also tend to feel happier and less worried about things. Friends can help people improve their feelings of self-esteem and self-worth — they make us feel good about ourselves and can help us get through challenging times.

Friendships help us to build resilience. Being able to share life's ups and downs with someone else makes it easier to deal with difficult things that happen in our lives. Talking things through with a close friend can help you learn to solve problems and resolve conflicts with others. You also get to practice how to ask for help, which is an important life skill.

Friends also help us deal with stress — those uncomfortable feelings we might get when we are worried or scared about something. When you have a good friend, you can work through your worries with someone who cares about you. Talking with someone about your feelings, dreams, and fears can be very powerful.

Friendships promote kindness. They help us learn to empathize with others and have compassion for them.

This means that we can really understand and care for the feelings of others. Compassion, empathy, and kindness will all be key to developing a happy and fulfilling life in the long run, and friendships are a great place to practice these skills.

WHAT MAKES A GREAT FRIEND?

In order to make friends, you need learn how to be a great friend yourself. Well, how do you do that? We'll give some pointers here.

Great Friends Support Each Other

Do and say things that make your friends feel good. You can compliment or congratulate them when they share their accomplishments with you. Remember what your friends like—maybe a favorite song or snack—so that you can surprise them with it every now and then. Being thoughtful, remembering what makes your friends happy, and then trying to share that happiness with them will make your friends feel good, and showing them kindness will probably make you feel good too.

Everyone feels down sometimes, and during those times, we really need our friends. If your friend is feeling down, support them. If there is something safe and easy you can do to help them out, then you might want to do that. If you don't know how to help, try to connect your friend with an adult who might know how to help, such as a teacher or parent.

Great Friends are Not Always Similar

Almost everyone has a hobby or interest that they enjoy. Even if you don't like the same things as your friend, a great friend encourages instead of criticizing. You might not enjoy a TV show that your friend likes, or they might not like listening to the same music as you. That is okay! Good friends understand that sometimes each person needs to do their own thing, and other times friends can enjoy doing things they both enjoy together.

Great Friends Listen

When you are talking with a friend, be careful not to interrupt them. Listen carefully to what they're saying so you can be sure you understand their feelings. You can ask questions to make sure you understand and to show that you really care about what they have to say.

Great Friends are Trustworthy

Trusting a friend means you can believe what they tell you, and you can feel confident that they want what is best for you. Trust between friends can include things like not sharing private information about friends with anyone else unless you have the friend's permission to do so. It also means being reliable—if you tell a friend you will meet them after school, then you should be there on time so that your friend can trust that you will do what you say.

Trust can also mean keeping secrets, but sometimes this gets a little bit tricky. Sometimes people might share secrets that make you feel worried or scared. If that ever happens, it is best to talk with an adult about the situation. You can tell your friend, "This secret makes me feel uncomfortable and I need to talk with my mom about it." Your friend might not be happy about that, but sometimes it is necessary to include an adult who can make sure everyone is safe.

Great Friends Handle Conflict Respectfully and Respect Boundaries

Sometimes you might disagree with your friend about something. Other times, you might say or do something that upsets them. Good friends tell you if you've hurt them and apologize when they've done something wrong. In Chapter 3, we will discuss communication and conflict in more detail.

A Great Friendship Goes Both Ways

Friendships aren't good if one person always talks and the other always listens, or if one person is always supportive while the other is not. When friends are kind to one another, both feel good and feel supported. In a good friendship, both friends contribute to each other's happiness. If you are not feeling this way in a friendship, some of the tips in Chapter 4 might help you to have a conversation about this with your friend.

Great Friends are Not Just Followers

On social media, you might feel pressured to gain followers and social media "friends," but these are not the same kind of friends we're talking about in this book. These are more like your casual acquaintances — or sometimes even total strangers — and not the true, supportive, caring friends who will help you get through life. Save your most precious and private thoughts for the people who care about you because you only need a handful of friends for true happiness.

HAVE A GROUP
OF FRIENDS

Don't limit yourself to one "best friend." Some people like having lots of friends, while for others just a few will do. Either way is fine. Share your friendship with everyone you enjoy spending time with and who treats you with kindness. Having a variety of different friends will give you people to explore different interests with, and allow you to learn lots of new things. Having a group of friends makes it more likely that you'll always have someone to lean on when you need it.

UNRELIABLE
FRIENDS

Sometimes you may realize someone you thought was a friend has not been kind or loyal to you. This can be a painful experience, and, unfortunately, it is bound to happen sometimes.

While your feelings may be hurt, try to carefully describe to the person how their behavior has affected you. Say something like, "I'm upset that you kicked me out of the group chat," or "It hurts my feelings when you say bad things about my hair." Make sure they know what you want from them, such as setting a boundary to not bring up certain topics.

A true friend will regret making you feel bad, apologize sincerely, and try to avoid ever doing that hurtful thing again. If they're sincere, their behavior will change, and your friendship can continue, having survived this challenge.

On the other hand, you may find that the person does not apologize sincerely, says you are overreacting, or even blames you for how you have handled the situation. This person's behavior may not change, even after you've explained how they've hurt your feelings. If this is the case, this person is not a friend, and you should probably take your friendship elsewhere.

CHAPTER TWO:

GETTING TO
KNOW PEOPLE

Now that you know what a friend is, and what the benefits of friendship are, let's talk about getting to know people and some tips for making new friends. In this chapter, we'll talk about three steps you can take to get to know people—finding common ground, taking it slow, and meeting new people through the friends you already have.

FIND COMMON GROUND

Participate in your favorite activities, such as clubs, sports teams, or music groups. You may also want to find places to volunteer in your city or town, perhaps distributing food or caring for animals in a shelter. There are probably places where you can volunteer your time to work while making a difference and learning about whatever issues you care about. These are all great ways to meet new people while doing an activity that you enjoy or exploring a new interest. If you don't know where to start when you're looking for activities to join, ask an adult at home or school to help you.

If you meet a friend through school or an outside activity, you already have some common ground you can build on. Talk about things you like or don't like about school or your shared activity, then ask them about other things they like to do. You already know you have at least one thing in common, and that commonality provides you with good topics for your first conversations.

If you find out you have other common interests, great! If your new friend is involved in activities that you're not involved in, but are interesting to you, ask about them. It might be a good way for you to find a new activity to get involved in and possibly meet even more new friends.

BE PROACTIVE

Being proactive means making an effort to achieve your goal rather than waiting for it to happen. There are many ways you can be proactive about building friendships. Joining activities and volunteering your time, as mentioned above, are great ways to be proactive about meeting new people. In addition, being proactive in your communication will help the new people you meet become true friends.

Use Body Language to Communicate That You Are Open to Friendship

When you're meeting someone new, maybe in a class or at a new activity you've joined, use your body language to show that you are friendly and want to talk. When we cross our arms or avoid eye contact, it can send a message that we don't really want to talk to people. To be welcoming, try not to cross your arms or legs and make friendly eye contact with the people around you.

Practice holding your head high and relaxing your shoulders — this shows others that you are open to talking and friendship.

Make an Effort

Don't wait for others to talk, ask you questions, or suggest a time to get together. You can be the first one to do all of these things! Introduce yourself, ask questions to get to know new people, and don't be afraid to ask your new friends if they want to meet up. If you feel nervous about doing these things, the other person probably does too! You can help a friendship develop by being the first one to reach out.

TAKE IT SLOW

When making new friends, take it slow. Don't expect a new friend to spend every minute with you, and don't take it personally if some time passes without hearing from them. Spend some time with them one day, then give them a day or two, then see if they want to do something together again in a few days. It is natural for new friendships to take some time to really grow.

MEET NEW PEOPLE THROUGH THE FRIENDS YOU ALREADY HAVE

A new friend can be a great way to meet even more people. If you get along with the other people your new friend knows, great! If not, that's okay too. We talked above about the benefits of having a group of friends, but in reality, many people have several different groups of friends. We might have our school friends, who are different than our neighborhood friends, who are different from the friends we hang out with at soccer or church. Having all of these different people to support you in different areas of your life is terrific. So if you and a new friend happen to belong to the same larger group of friends, that is great, but don't worry if that's not the case. You can each have your separate friends, too.

CHOOSE GOOD FRIENDS

Always remember—you deserve good friends. You only want to be friends with people who make you feel good, and you can avoid those who don't.

QUESTIONS TO
ASK YOURSELF

1. How can you build common ground with other kids based on your interests?
2. What different areas of your life could lead to different groups of friends?
3. How will you introduce yourself to a new person, and what are some questions you could ask to get to know them?

What part of the process of making friends makes you the most nervous? That would be the part it will be helpful for you to practice. You can practice introducing yourself, asking questions, and more in front of a mirror until you feel comfortable with what you might want to say to a new friend.

CHAPTER THREE:
HANDLING STRONG EMOTIONS

As humans, we need relationships with others. We rely on others for help, safety, companionship, and fun. Having strong bonds with family and friends has been shown to help people live longer, and it definitely makes life more enjoyable. There are so many benefits to having strong relationships, but sometimes they can be difficult as well.

When we interact with others, those interactions can lead to very strong feelings. Sometimes these are positive feelings — laughter, love, happiness, and intimacy. But sometimes, they are negative feelings, like anger, frustration, and disappointment.

These types of feelings come up every now and then, even in the strongest relationships, so it's not realistic to try to avoid negative feelings altogether. However, there are some ways you can manage these feelings to make them easier to resolve. Managing strong feelings takes a lot of time and practice. Don't expect yourself to become calm all of a sudden! The strategies below are ones you can practice over time, and they'll come in handy not only in your friendships but in many areas of your life.

EVERYONE HAS FEELINGS!

Remember that everyone has feelings and that sometimes dealing with strong emotions can be difficult. Strong feelings are harder to handle in public than at home, but many of the strategies below are ones you can use anytime, anywhere.

Everyone has strong feelings sometimes, and everyone worries sometimes. No worry or feeling is weird, and you don't need to feel alone with your emotions. When you share your worries with someone you trust, it always makes it better. The same goes for sad and lonely feelings. Let them out rather than holding them inside.

DEEP BREATHING

When you feel very strong feelings, you can calm them through deep breathing. This may help you think more clearly so that you can decide what to do next.

Start by taking three deep breaths from your belly. Try counting slowly to four while you breathe in, holding your breath for a second or two, and then counting all the way to eight while you breathe out. Do this several times until you feel calmer. It is most calming if you can do this by breathing through your nose.

BEWARE OF
OVERREACTIONS

Assess your feelings according to the situation. Sometimes we feel things more strongly than is actually necessary. If your friend ate the last cookie, you might feel disappointed and sigh, which would be appropriate. But if you screamed and yelled, that would be an oversized reaction. Most situations tend to be pretty minor, so double-check whether you are overreacting.

DESCRIBE YOUR
FEELINGS

Talking about feelings aloud can be very helpful. If you have a friend or trusted adult nearby, try to explain to them which emotions you are feeling. Are you angry, scared, frustrated, disappointed, sad, embarrassed, or something else? The more specific you can be about which emotion you are feeling, the more relief you might experience from talking about it.

Using "I" statements is a great way to express your feelings. We'll cover these in more detail in Chapter 4, but basically these are statements like "I feel _____ when_____, because _____, and I need, like, wish, or prefer _____." For example, "I feel very frustrated when someone isn't following the rules, because it isn't fair, and I need for us to check the rules."

Some people also like to write about their feelings, for example, in a journal. That is another terrific way to name your emotions, describe how they feel, and think through what you'd like to do about them.

OWN YOUR FEELINGS

One useful thing to remember is that only you are in control of your feelings. No one else can get into your head to see if you feel mad, sad, or happy. We have these emotions in response to how we perceive situations, but ultimately how you interpret a situation and feel about it is up to you. Take ownership over your feelings so that you can best decide how you want to move forward.

CRYING

Everyone cries sometimes. Sometimes tears well up when you're sad, disappointed, or hurt, and that's okay. Sometimes, crying actually helps us to feel much better. Just like talking or writing in a journal, for some people crying is a way to get their feelings out rather than keeping them all stuck inside, and that is a good thing.

However, you may feel like you don't want to cry in front of other people, especially your friends. It can be tough to stop tears when you can feel them coming, but some of the strategies below may help. You can use these strategies when you are in a situation where it doesn't feel comfortable or safe to cry, to buy yourself some time. Then you can let those tears flow when you get to a place that is more private.

Slow and silent breathing. Just like we discussed above, count four seconds in your head — "One thousand, two thousand..." as you inhale, hold your breath for a count of four seconds, and then gently exhale for eight seconds. Continue to do this until you feel more settled and in control of your emotions.

Distract yourself. Shift your attention to something else for a little while, just to get your mind off of whatever is making you start to cry. Count ceiling tiles, do math in your head, or mentally list all your relatives and classmates in your class.

Take a break. Occasionally, it's best to remove yourself from a situation. Get a drink of water or take a short trip to the bathroom and imagine yourself rinsing your upset feelings away as you wash your hands.

COMFORT YOURSELF

An even better way to calm yourself when things go wrong is to try not to get too upset in the first place. The way that we talk to ourselves affects how we feel, and being able to comfort ourselves during hard times is an important skill.

Positive Self-Talk

Think of a time when you did something wrong or said something wrong. What thoughts did you have, or what did you say to yourself? You probably talked negatively to yourself. That kind of talk can make the situation worse. A better way to handle the situation would have been to find a way to comfort yourself.

For example, if you were in a spelling bee and got a hard word wrong, you could have said something to yourself like, "It's okay, that was a hard word," or "Everyone messes up sometimes." You can even pat yourself on the back and say, "Wow, I was so brave to do this spelling bee, and I made it pretty far!" Say the same things to yourself that you would say to your friends to encourage them. If your friends were upset, you wouldn't tell them they did a terrible job, so don't tell yourself that either.

Use Coping Thoughts

As well as comforting yourself, coping thoughts can help you deal with a difficult situation. You can't completely trick yourself into thinking, "This is great!" But, if you aren't convinced it is, you can still use coping thoughts to give yourself a boost.

For example, you could say, "I don't like this, but I'll get through it," or "I've dealt with hard things before," or "It won't last long," or "I'm strong enough to handle this." Most of the time, bad events are just a bump in the road of life, and you can get past them.

Moving Away from Bad Feelings

Feeling sad or angry when something bad happens is natural, and you'll want to deal with those emotions, but don't get stuck in those feelings for the long term. Once you've done what you can to address the problem—maybe telling a friend that your feelings were hurt or finding an adult who can help—you'll need to let yourself move on and leave this problem behind you. Don't keep carrying it around once you've done what you could to resolve it.

Sometimes moving on means taking action so that things will be better next time. For example, if you don't do well at one spelling bee, have your mom or dad quiz you so you feel more confident at the next one. Sometimes you can't do anything about a bad event, so do something pleasant instead to be kind to yourself. Play a game with a friend, cook dinner with your parents, listen to music, or read a favorite book. What are some other ways you can you cope when you feel upset?

CHAPTER FOUR:
SPEAKING UP
WITH FRIENDS

Good friends share their thoughts and feelings with each other. That's how they get to know one another better, and all of that communication is what builds a real friendship. However, as you may already know, it's not always easy to get your point across. Sometimes we worry about what others might think of our opinions, or we just can't find the right words to say how we feel.

When we are upset, we sometimes express our thoughts and feelings very strongly. Yelling, calling other people names, or crying might be honest reactions, but they aren't usually productive communication, especially between friends. This chapter is about speaking up to say what you mean without being mean.

BE TRUE TO YOURSELF

Sometimes you may choose to stay silent rather than disagree with someone, and you might think this silence is a nice thing to do. It's good to care about other people's feelings, but you have the right to express your own feelings as well, even when they're different from your friend's.

Use "I" Statements to Set the Right Tone

One way to state your thoughts and feelings without accidentally being too harsh toward others is to use "I" statements. "I" statements are sentences that begin with the word "I" and describe what you feel without criticizing anyone else.

"I" statements can solve problems by helping friends talk about disagreements without blaming each other. When you use "I" to start your statement, you're giving your point of view while recognizing that your friend might see things differently. You say, "I feel X when X happens…" It is really important that you do not blame the other person for how you feel.

Instead of….	Try…..
"You make me so angry!"	"I feel angry when I am yelled at."
"You're so annoying!"	"I'm feeling squished. Could you move over a bit?"

After you make an "I" statement, you could make a polite request, like in the second example.

Say "No" When Needed

There are times when you have to say "no" to your friends. You can say no in a lot of different ways, according to the situation. You could say things like:

"I'm not comfortable doing that."

"If I did that, my mother would be angry with me."

"No, thanks."

"That's not something I enjoy doing."

"I don't want to do that. Let's do something else instead."

"I don't like that idea."

"I really don't want to do that."

"I don't feel like doing that."

It may be difficult to say no at first, especially if you must say it several times, but it gets easier with practice. If you're not sure whether to say yes or no, take some time to think things over. Tell your friend you need to think about it, and you'll let them know later. Then make sure to let your friend know what you decide.

HANDLING FRIENDSHIP
ROUGH SPOTS

Every friendship has occasional friendship rough spots. A rough spot occurs when friends unintentionally hurt each other's feelings. When a friendship is mostly good, it's not wise or kind to end it over a rough spot. Instead, there are ways to move past that bad moment successfully.

Sometimes we try to make a joke, but it doesn't come out right. Or we try to tease someone in a friendly way, but their feelings get hurt. These types of misunderstandings happen to us all, and it's important to learn how to notice when something has gone wrong with your communication so that you can repair the damage.

Notice Stop Signals

When you are talking with others, pay attention to stop signals. Stop signals are signs that something might have gone wrong in communication, and it needs to be fixed before you can move forward.

People sometimes use words — either polite ones or angry ones — to tell you to stop. Sometimes stop signals are communicated by someone's facial expression or body language. For example, maybe your friend rolls their eyes, frowns, crosses their arms, or turns away from you. These all might be clues that you need to check in with your friend to make sure there hasn't been a miscommunication.

Which of the following sentences contain stop signals?

1. Quit it!
2. What time is it?
3. My sister has brown eyes.
4. Cut it out!
5. You're being annoying!
6. No, I'm in fourth grade, not third.
7. Please don't call me that.
8. Be quiet.

Answers: 1, 4, 5, 7, and 8. Even though 6 has the word "no" in it, it's a clarification, not a stop signal.

If a friend starts teasing you, you have a few options of ways you can react. You can play along with the teasing, or you can politely ask them to stop. For example, if you're wearing something your friend says looks funny, you could make a joke about how funny it looks, or you could ask them to please stop teasing because it bothers you.

If you choose the second option, and your friend is truly your friend, they should honor your request.

Remember from Chapter 1 — great friends trust each other, and this means trusting your friend to be kind and to stop doing things that bother you. When something bothers you, it is always best to mention it, so your friend will know not to do it again in the future.

Likewise, when a friend speaks up and tells you that you've done something that bothers them, then it's your turn to be respectful and honor their request to stop.

Say You're Sorry When You Offend Someone

Whenever you say or do something that annoys or upsets someone, stop immediately. Then simply say, "I'm sorry." Right away, this indicates that you didn't hurt them on purpose and would like to try to fix it. Just saying you're sorry might not be enough to fully solve a problem, but it is always a good place to start.

Sometimes your friend might be upset or hurt by something that you said or did, but you don't think you did anything wrong. For example, maybe you said something as a joke that accidentally hurt your friend's feelings. You might think they are being too sensitive, and you don't think you need to apologize for the joke. These differences of opinion sometimes happen between friends. At times like this, saying "I'm sorry" is still the right thing to do. You are apologizing for hurting their feelings and making them feel bad.

Give the Benefit of the Doubt

When we feel nervous or self-conscious, we may start to worry that others don't like us or that they are gossiping about us behind our backs. Most of the time, this isn't true. It's an act of kindness to believe the best about your friends. Most people are kind most of the time, especially those who have already shown they are good friends to you. So if you see them whispering, don't assume it's about you. You can always ask your friends if you are really worried. Often, whatever a friend does to upset another friend is just an accident or a misunderstanding. Considering possible explanations other than deliberate unkindness could help you avoid overreacting. Until you know they've done something unkind for sure, try to give them the benefit of the doubt.

They're Probably Not Trying to Be Mean

It's rare for people to be mean on purpose, especially if they're your friends.

What if you do hear someone say something mean about you? Should you confront them? Probably not. They'll just deny it or get mad at you for accusing them. If they aren't talking directly to you, it's best not to respond to them in any way.

It's hard to accept, but we can't control what other people say about us. We can't tape their mouths shut.

When you demand that others stop talking about you, you promote gossip. It gives people even more to whisper about. Pretend the gossip doesn't bother you and let the mean comments fade away. This is very hard to do. You might feel upset inside, but don't show how you feel to the gossipers because seeing you hurt or angry makes them feel powerful. You may want to remember that the people who know and care about you won't believe the bad things those people say about you anyway.

If you find certain people often say mean things about you, you may need to hang out with kinder friends.

HANDLING UNKIND BEHAVIOR

Trying to distinguish between teasing and bullying can be tricky, so let's start by clarifying what each of these words mean. Teasing is when you poke fun at a person. It can be playful and affectionate between friends, or it can be unkind and hurtful.

Bullying refers to deliberate acts of meanness aimed at a specific person that are repeated over a period of time. Bullies often try to make themselves seem bigger, stronger, or somehow more powerful than the person who's being bullied, which makes it difficult for the person being bullied to stand up for themselves.

Sometimes bullying can be physical, involving pushing or fighting, but it does not have to be. Calling someone names, spreading lies or bad stories about a person, or intentionally excluding someone from activities can also be forms of bullying. Bullying can also happen online, which is called cyberbullying.

Responding to Teasing

As we have discussed, teasing can be hurtful. Sometimes teasing is mean on purpose, and sometimes it is mean accidentally, like when someone is trying to make a joke, for example. When someone teases you in a way you don't like, use the strategies above to let them know that it bothers you. Most people — including friends — will apologize and not tease you that way again.

Unfortunately, sometimes people tease on purpose, and they don't want to stop even when they know it hurts others people's feelings. Your friends should not do this to you — this is not the behavior of a true friend. If you do have a friend who behaves this way, you may need to consider distancing yourself from that person and finding new friends who are more kind.

You may encounter unkind teasing from people who are not your friends, like other kids at school who you don't know very well. This is an uncomfortable, difficult situation to handle, and it's okay to feel nervous and upset about it. Talk to your friends and trusted adults about those feelings.

Here are some strategies you can consider for when someone teases you and does not stop, even after you tell them it hurts your feelings.

Ignore

You may choose to simply ignore teasing. The person teasing you is not your friend and is not being respectful of your feelings, so you may choose to ignore them altogether. Why bother trying to argue with them when they've already shown that they don't care what you say or how you feel? Ignoring is a fine choice if it feels right for you and your situation.

Sometimes ignoring can be a good strategy when people are very unkind. Sometimes, trying to argue or getting very upset can make people tease you even more. So if you've already tried speaking up against someone who is teasing and it seemed to make it worse, you might want to try ignoring them instead. Also, make sure you are involving trusted adults in this situation. No one deserves to be consistently teased, and adults should help you solve this problem.

Stay Close to Others

Another way to deal with teasing is to stay near a grown-up or a group of your friends. There is safety in numbers, and other people are less likely to be mean to you when you're surrounded by supportive and kind people.

Point Out Meanness

When faced with teasing or any form of unkindness, whether you're with friends or just acquaintances, you always have the great option to simply point out that what is happening is mean. By naming something out loud as mean, or rude, and doing so calmly and clearly, you are identifying the situation for everyone around you. You're probably saying something that many other people are thinking too!

When pointing out meanness, don't shout, but feel free to make it loud enough that an adult can hear. You should speak calmly and matter-of-factly. Just the same way you would say, "two plus two equals four," you can say, "That was a mean thing to say." Or, "You know, that was really rude." After that, walk away from the mean person.

Since most kids don't like to think of themselves as mean, pointing out their meanness right away could discourage them from being mean again. Teachers or other kids may also help you.

Dealing with Bullying

Sometimes, unkindness goes beyond teasing and becomes bullying. The difference between these two can be difficult to figure out sometimes, since teasing and bullying are closely related.

You can think about teasing as something that happens once — a kid teases you about your hairstyle. It becomes bullying when it happens repeatedly — that same kid teases you about your hairstyle or something else every day. If you start to feel afraid of someone, or notice that you go out of your way to avoid seeing them because you are afraid they will tease you again, then you are probably dealing with a bully.

Bullies pick on people for many reasons. Most of the reasons actually have nothing to do with you — the target of the bullying. Most of the reasons have to do with the bullies themselves, and whatever they are nervous or upset about. So try really hard not to take bullying personally, even though that can be hard to do sometimes.

Bullies may choose their target because they think that person will be easy to bully. By being assertive and using the strategies to respond to teasing that we discussed above (say no, ignore, use humor, point out meanness), you might be able to protect yourself from some bullying.

But often, there isn't much a kid can do to stop a bully. Do not feel like it is your job to take care of a bully or make them change their behavior. This is really a situation where an adult needs to step in.

Asking an adult for help with a bully is not being a tattletale or being weak. In fact, it takes strength and maturity to ask for help in these situations. You are standing up for yourself and for others. Bringing the problem to an adult's attention is usually the only way to solve a bullying issue, so you can be proud of yourself for actually taking steps to fix the problem.

How to Tell an Adult about Bullying

Don't announce to the bully that you are going to tell an adult. If you yell, "I'm telling!" it could anger a bully even more. Instead, step away from the situation and then figure out which adults you will speak to about the bullying. Bring a friend with you for comfort and support if that makes it easier.

When the bully isn't around, tell your parents, teachers, or someone else who you trust. Describe what you've already done to handle the situation so they understand that this is beyond your abilities. Your safety is their responsibility.

Reporting bullying can be intimidating for kids because they fear making the situation worse. The bully may have threatened them with further injury if they told an adult. Tell an adult anyway. Bullying isn't okay for anyone, including you.

If you tell an adult and they don't seem very helpful—maybe they don't believe you about the bullying, or they say something unhelpful like, "You are being too sensitive"—then tell someone else. Even if it's hard or scary, keep telling until an adult steps in to stop the bullying.

Whenever you can't protect yourself, the adults in your life must do so. When you're being bullied, what can adults do to help protect you?

- They can talk to the kid or kids doing the bullying and insist that they stop.
- They can make the bully or bullies apologize and do something to make up for their behavior.
- They can talk to the parents of the kids doing the bullying.
- They can talk to the followers of the kids doing the bullying to convince them not to go along with it.
- They can provide more supervision or remove privileges from kids doing the bullying so there's less opportunity for the bullying to continue.
- They can get other kids involved in making sure you are protected from bullying.

- They can offer programs to teach your whole school or community about ways to prevent bullying.

Bullying only continues and often gets worse when it's kept secret. If a bully's secrets are revealed, then they lose their power.

Standing Up for a Friend Who's Being Bullied

What if it's your friend who's being bullied? The fear of being picked on makes many friends afraid to speak up in such a situation.

The best way you can help your friend is to tell a caring adult what's going on. For your friend's safety, you may need to involve a grown-up even if your friend asks you not to. As a good friend, you should speak up when you or your friends need adult assistance.

Questions for this Chapter

1. Do you have any examples of situations where you should speak up but haven't so far? Is there anything holding you back from speaking up?

2. Are you guilty of yelling at your friends or calling them names? How did your friends respond? What could you have done instead?

3. When you're feeling frustrated, it's tempting to yell. What's wrong with communicating this way?

4. Do you tend to apologize when you haven't done anything wrong? Has anyone told you to stop apologizing? A sincere apology can help resolve a conflict, but too much apologizing can be irritating. Can you explain why?

5. Can you explain why it's sometimes hard to say no to a friend? Have you ever agreed to something your friend wanted but later regretted it? Which of the ways to say no would be easiest for you to use with a friend?

6. Have you ever been teased at school? How did you react? What would be the easiest way for you to respond to teasing?

7. Can you think of a situation where a trusted grown-up could help you or a friend who was being bullied?

CHAPTER FIVE:
FRIENDSHIP CONFLICTS

In the previous chapter, we talked about responding to unkindness, like teasing. Hopefully, you won't need to confront unkindness too often. In this chapter, we will talk about the smaller conflicts that can happen between friends and how to handle them productively.

Sometimes, you and your friends will disagree or annoy each other. There may be times when playing together isn't fun, or your friends just don't want to do what you want them to do. But friendship rough spots don't have to be the end of a friendship. In this chapter, we'll talk about accepting when things aren't going your way or when people won't act the way you want them to. You will learn how to deal with everyday problems that happen between friends.

RESPECT OTHERS' CHOICES

Sometimes kids act like they are the boss, and they get to make all the decisions about what to do and how to do it. You may have encountered a friend, sibling, or classmate like this in the past. They may say things like, "It has to be this way," or "You can't do that!" or "Because I said so." You might even be the one who does this sometimes! While it can be tempting to try to make up all the rules for other people to follow, you need to know that this behavior is usually annoying to others. Maybe you have felt annoyed when someone has done this to you. It's not a good way to interact with friends.

Instead of trying to make up and enforce all of the rules, we all have to compromise and accept other people's choices sometimes, even when we disagree with them. When you are with a friend, make sure that each of you has a chance to make some of the decisions. Don't just think about what you want, but also think about what is kind and fair. A good strategy to use is to ask questions instead of giving orders.

Also, remember that it's not your job to make sure other kids behave well — let the grown-ups do that.

TELLING VS. TATTLING

Sometimes, kids try to get other kids in trouble in order to get their own way or to get attention from adults. We often call this tattling, or being a tattletale. If you have siblings at home, you might be familiar with this behavior, as it is pretty common among children. But just because something happens a lot does not mean it's right or a good way to get along with people.

When you are with your friends, try your best to resolve any conflicts or hurt feelings between yourselves by talking it through. You probably don't need to tell an adult every time a friend does something that annoys or bothers you. In most of these situations, you will be able to solve the conflict on your own, and working through those problems is how friendships actually get stronger.

But there are some times when you do need to tell an adult what is going on with a friend. Make sure to tell an adult if:

- Someone is hurt or might get hurt.
- Something is broken or might get broken.
- You tried to handle a difficult situation on your own, but you haven't been able to solve it.
- Someone is very upset and cannot calm down.
- Any other situation that is unsafe or that you feel unable to handle well on your own.

Figure it Out

When does it seem like it would be a good idea to tell a grown-up?

1. Bo is chewing gum at school.
2. Alexis cut in front of you in line.
3. Carlin is throwing a ball at the window.
4. Isaac is making annoying noises while you're trying to work. You've asked him twice to stop, but he keeps doing it.
5. Ying fell down on the playground and is crying.
6. Kiersten took the blue marker, and you want to use it.

7. Gabriela saved a seat in the cafeteria for her friend, which is against the rules.
8. Some big boys keep tossing around a little boy's lunch box.

Answers: 3, 5, and 8 are situations where you need to tell an adult because there's possible danger. Situation 4 is also a situation where you may want to ask for help because you've tried but haven't been able to handle it on your own.

Remember, telling an adult should be something you do to get help, not to get someone else in trouble.

MOVE PAST CONFLICT

Have you ever felt stuck with a bad memory of a friend who treated you poorly? Maybe you keep thinking about something they did that you didn't like, and you can't seem to forget it or forgive them for it. That's called holding a grudge. A grudge means staying mad at someone for something that happened in the past. People often hold grudges against someone who does not even realize what they've done wrong.

All friendships have conflicts. Conflicts happen when two people disagree about something. Because no two people always think the same way, every friendship has disagreements. There will probably be times when you and your friend do things that annoy each other since no one is perfect.

Whether the friendship can continue will depend on how you handle the conflict. Conflict isn't pleasant, but if you handle it well, working through conflict can strengthen your friendship by helping you understand each other better.

Don't pull out of a friendship without giving the other person a chance to make things better. You can handle conflict with your friends in the following ways:

- Give your friend another chance.

- Ask for what you want.
- Accept the way your friend is.
- Do something different together.

Some of these are "inside" strategies because they involve how you think about the situation in your own mind, and others are "outside" strategies that involve talking directly to your friend. It's not always necessary to take action when faced with a problem. There are times when changing your perspective is the best way to deal with it. If you decide to talk to your friend about a problem, maybe because it happens too often or because it bothers you a lot, express your concerns in a way your friend can accept.

HOW NOT TO TALK
ABOUT A PROBLEM

There are a few ways you should NOT talk to a friend about a problem. We'll discuss those in this section.

Yelling and Calling Names

When you feel angry, it's tempting to turn up the volume. However, your friends aren't going to want to listen to what you're saying when you yell, and they'll probably yell back. Having a shouting match definitely doesn't solve a problem. It just makes loud noise, and it could make the problem worse. Also, calling someone names is mean. It's hurtful and not helpful.

Bringing Up Old Issues

If you decide to bring up an issue with a friend, do it right when it first happens, or within a day or two. That will allow you to talk through and resolve the problem right away, rather than letting it grow into a grudge over time.

When you are talking through a problem with a friend, it's best to focus on just one issue at a time. Sometimes kids think that if they build up their courage to bring up one problem, they should mention all of them at the same time. For example, maybe today you are upset with your friend because you let them borrow your favorite pen and they lost it. This is upsetting, and you should tell your friend how you feel. But do not use this as an opportunity to say you're upset about the pen, and you're also upset about that time last week when they were late, and you're also upset about that time three weeks ago when they teased you about your shirt.

Bringing up all of these complaints or accusations at the same time will be overwhelming for your friend, and that will make it really difficult to actually solve any of those problems. Also, if someone feels like you are making a long list of everything they've done wrong, that might hurt *their* feelings and make the situation even worse. Now you're both upset!

So just focus on the issue at hand, the one that is happening now that you need to talk about, until it is solved.

Complaining About a Friend to Others

Talking about friends behind their back is not kind and is not a good way of being trustworthy for your friend. Sometimes you might want to get advice for how to handle a problem with a friend, but it's best to do this with an adult, not another kid who also knows your friend.

Bringing up friendship problems in front of others can lead to embarrassment or teasing, or to someone feeling left out or feeling like others are ganging up on them. None of that is pleasant, kind, or fair to you or your friend. No one wants to be criticized in front of others.

To solve a problem, talk directly but gently to your friend about one issue when you can speak privately.

BUT WHAT SHOULD YOU SAY?

Telling someone you don't like something they're doing is important but can be difficult. It can be hard to deliver what feels like criticism, and it's often hard for people to hear criticisms of themselves. But these conversations are necessary for building strong relationships. Think about how you would want a friend to talk with you if you had done something wrong. Then use that same calmness, patience, and kindness when you are trying to bring up a difficult topic with a friend.

THE BEST WAYS TO DISCUSS A PROBLEM WITH A FRIEND

Use Constructive Criticism

You are probably familiar with the idea of criticism. Criticism, or criticizing someone, means pointing out their flaws or mistakes. *Constructive* criticism, on the other hand, is providing feedback to someone about a weakness or mistake *specifically in order to help them and make things better.*

An example of criticism might be, "You have a terrible singing voice. I can't stand listening to it." — Ouch!

An example of constructive criticism might be, "You aren't that good at those high notes yet, but I bet if you keep working with the music teacher, you will be able to reach them soon!" — Much better! You're still saying that someone isn't good at singing, but in a supportive way that's designed to show there is room for improvement.

Use a Soft Approach

Rather than being really direct, angry, or accusatory with a friend when pointing out a problem, you can take a softer approach that makes it easier for them to hear what you're saying.

This might mean excusing their behavior so that your focus is on how to make things better rather than focusing on what went wrong.

For example, you might say:

- "I'm sure you didn't mean to…"
- "You probably didn't realize…"
- "I know you were trying to…"
- "I understand it's hard for you to…"

Starting out this way tells your friend, "I know you're still a good person, even when you mess up."

After starting with a soft, supportive opening, you'll need to explain the problem. Describe clearly what your friend did that you didn't like and how it affected you. For example, "When you laughed at me after I fell down, it really hurt my feelings."

Then, ask for what you want. Use a phrase like "Could you please…" or "Next time can we…" so that your focus stays on fixing things for the future rather than dwelling on the past.

In the scenario where a friend laughs after you trip and fall, the whole statement could go like this:

"I know it probably looked funny, and you didn't mean to be mean, but when you laughed at me, it really hurt my feelings. Next time, could you try not to laugh and just help me up?"

Here is the formula you can use:

1. Use a soft, supportive opening.
2. Explain the specific problem.
3. Ask for what you want to be different in the future.

Apologize For Your Part in the Conflict

One effective way to handle conflict is to begin with soft criticism. Another way is to apologize. Conflict between friends always has two sides to the story. It is possible that your friend did or said something less than kind, but it is possible that you did as well. Sincere apologies can help you get past a friendship rough spot.

You don't seem sincere just by saying sorry, especially if you yell or mutter it. Don't be afraid to tell your friend specifically what you're sorry for doing. Don't use "but," because it takes away from your apology. "I'm sorry, but…" sounds like you're not really sorry. And don't blame your friend for what you did wrong.

If you can, apologize or promise to do things differently from now on. Usually, when you apologize to a friend, they will also apologize to you. But even if they don't, you'll know that you did the right thing to try to mend the friendship.

The Power of Forgiveness

So far, we've talked about handling conflict by talking things out with your friend. Occasionally, however, it is best to just forgive a friend. If you keep a mental list of every bad thing your friend has ever done, you are hurting yourself by carrying those feelings in your heart. Not only does forgiveness benefit your friend, but it benefits you as well since you will have more energy to focus on more important things.

Forgiveness is a generous thing to do. Forgiveness does not mean denying what happened. Simply accept that everyone makes mistakes and treat your friend the way you would like to be treated. It means letting go of anger because you care about your friend.

As a good friend, you don't hold grudges. These guidelines will assist you in determining when to forgive and forget:

Forgiveness Suggestions

- If it only happened one time, and it probably won't happen again, forget about it.
- If your friend didn't do it on purpose, forget about it.
- If it wasn't that bad, forget about it.
- If your friend is sorry, forget about it.
- If it was just a mistake, and the friend is usually kind, forget about it.
- If it happened more than a month ago, forget about it.

It is usually best to wait some time for tempers to cool before trying again. If you decide to forgive your friend, you don't have to announce it. Act friendly, smile, do something fun with your friend, or invite them over next time you see them.

WHEN FRIENDSHIPS END

Sometimes friendships end despite your best efforts. This happens to everyone. In some cases, friendships end in a big argument, but more often they simply fade away. It's natural for friends to drift apart when they are in different classes, change interests, or spend less time together.

One person deciding not to be friends while the other still wants to be friends is one of the most painful endings to a friendship. It is impossible to force someone to become your friend. You might have to let go of the idea of being friends with someone who rejects you repeatedly.

Losing a friend is always sad, but it isn't always a bad thing. When friends argue a lot or get into trouble together, they may benefit from separating. If spending time with someone is more painful than enjoyable, you might need to look for other friends.

The end of a friendship can cause you to feel upset, and that's understandable. It's hard to lose a friend. Someday, you might become good friends again if you were good friends before. However, remember that you don't have to remain alone.

Sometimes, letting go of one friendship allows room for other friendships to grow. Did you ever try something new and like it—maybe a new activity or ice cream flavor? The chances are that you never would have discovered how much you enjoy it if you hadn't been brave enough to try it. You may find the same thing to be true about a new friend.

Friendships are worth finding and keeping, whether they're with old friends or new ones. Therefore, you must let go of anger, sadness, and fear and hold on to the real caring that's at the heart of friendship.

Questions to Answer

Friendship means being flexible enough to accept when things don't go exactly how you want them to go. It also means being kind enough not to point out other people's mistakes in public or in a way that's hurtful to them. You learned to release grudges, let go of anger, and accept friends as they are.

1. Why should you avoid correcting someone in front of others?
2. Can you think of a time when you thought you were right, and your friend was wrong? What did you do, or what could you do, to resolve this disagreement?
3. Have you ever held a grudge about something the other person forgot about? How did holding on to it affect you? How did it affect the other person?
4. Have you ever done something that upset a friend? How did you feel afterward? Did your friend forgive you?
5. Have you ever had a friendship end? What happened?

6. How can you tell when you should let go of your anger and forgive a friend versus when you need to let go of a friendship and find different friends?

CHAPTER SIX:

BLENDING IN TO JOIN FRIENDS

It's great to have one-on-one friendships, but friendships between groups can be even more fun. Have you heard the saying "the more, the merrier?" More people means more excitement, ideas, and laughter. The problem with having more opinions is that they can also make it harder to play or work together.

Are you ever uncomfortable when others appear to be enjoying themselves? Would you be able to recall a time when you were part of a group project or sports team where you felt frustrated because people didn't cooperate? This part of the book talks about blending in. You will learn how to get along with partners or teammates, join a group, and contribute to a fun team environment.

THE SECRET TO
JOINING A GROUP

Have you ever watched the grown-ups in your life drive on a highway? First, they watch the traffic; then, they slide into it without interrupting the flow. In driving, this is called merging. Something similar occurs as you make friends.

What would happen if grown-ups just barged into the traffic flow without looking? There would be a big crash! Just barging in doesn't work with kids either. If you suddenly just join into a group, they might be mad at you for interrupting them. On the other hand, just watching and waiting without joining in doesn't get you anywhere, just like it doesn't get cars anywhere on the highway.

How to Merge

Joining a group of kids is just like drivers merging onto a highway—just watch, then blend. This means:

Stand near a group and watch what they're doing.

1. Then slide into the action without interrupting it.

So how do you use this strategy? First, you need to watch closely to understand how the group is playing or what they are trying to accomplish. When you're ready to blend, do something that adds to the play. Here are some possible ways to blend:

- Do the same thing the group is doing nearby, then gradually move closer.
- Give a compliment.
- Bring extra toys or supplies.
- Help them lift, carry, or get something so they can continue playing.
- Get in line to take a turn.

Isn't it Rude to Join Without Asking?

No, contributing without interfering is respectful.

What if the others won't let you join when you try to watch then blend? What if they say the game is private? It can happen. Even well-liked kids get left out sometimes, and you don't need to take it personally when it happens. But if you don't try to join in at all, you're guaranteed not to be part of the fun.

Joining a Game with Rules

So far, we've talked about how to join a group of kids who are just hanging out and playing. What is the best way to join a game with rules? If it's a short game or a two-player game, just watch and wait until it's finished and join the next round. You could say, "I'll play the winner!"

When a group is playing a sport, you can stand close by while they select teams. Or, if one team has fewer players, you could join the smaller team to make them more even.

Join the losing team if a game is already underway. Losing teams will be more open to your help than winning teams. Take advantage of a break in the action and do something that keeps the game moving. In the event that a ball goes off the field, you could run to get it and then join the team.

What if There's No Room in the Game?

Avoid pushing too hard if you try to join in and the other kids won't let you play. Getting angry and demanding won't help your cause, and it will likely make the group even more determined to keep you out. Keep smiling even if you do not feel pleasant. You could try to join a different group, or you could wait until later and try to join the first group again.

If you have tried two or three times to join a group, don't keep trying. Find another group that will include you. Also, leave behind a group that lets you join but then treats you badly and look for a different group.

Choosing Which Group to Join

When choosing a group, how do you decide? Get to know everyone in your age group and try to be friendly with them. In a strange situation with kids you don't know very well, it's a good idea to smile and be near them. For example, if you just started on a new soccer team and you recognize some kids from your school, you should definitely say hi and stand next to them for warm-up exercises.

It's polite to say hello to people you know. This is a good first step to joining their group. Whether a friendship develops from that point forward is up to you, but you don't want to eliminate the possibility by staying away from the start. When you act as if you don't know someone, you come across as unfriendly.

What about people you do know well? When it comes to joining a friendship group, how do you decide? Here are some questions to consider:

- Do you like doing the same things they do?
- Have they shown signs they enjoy your company? (For example, do they smile when they see you or include you when they make plans?)
- Do you feel good when you're with them?
- Do you have fun together?
- Are they usually kind to you?
- Do your parents and teachers seem to like them?

You may not be a good fit for that group if you answered "no" to several of these questions. Sometimes kids stick with a social group who are often mean to them because they think they don't have any other choice. But there's always another choice. Moving away from a familiar group is hard, but it's better to do that than allow yourself to be treated badly.

You don't have to belong just to one group. It's fun and interesting to have more than one circle of friends. It gives you more options and lets you do different things with different friends. For example, you might enjoy playing sports with one group of friends, talking with another, and doing school projects with a third group.

CHANGING FRIENDSHIP GROUPS

Sometimes people switch friendship groups because of changing interests or situations. They might spend more time with one group and less time with another. There's nothing unusual or wrong about that.

When your friend switches friendship groups, it's hard to be left behind. But clinging and arguing will only push your friend further away. You might want to join your friend's new group. If not, consider spending more time with a different group. Stay on good terms, and your friend may join your group again after a while.

When moving away from an old group of friends, don't be mean about it. Don't criticize or tell your old group you don't like them anymore. Don't talk negatively about them to the new group.

Stay friendly with your old group while building a connection with the new one. Staying friends with your old group is possible even if you spend less time together. Keeping in touch with your old group ensures you have friends to play with even if the new group isn't as nice as you expected.

IMPROVING CONVERSATION SKILLS

When making friends, work on improving your conversation skills. Start by matching the tone of a conversation. This means when there's a conversation going on, pick up on the feeling of it and make a comment that has a similar feeling.

Whenever possible, make enthusiastic comments about a conversation's subject, without lying. You don't have to say you like what the other kids are talking about if you don't, but match their feelings.

Ask what the book is about instead of criticizing what they are talking about. Or ask if they have seen any other shows or books you might like.

When joining a group of kids, you don't need to sound exactly like them to make friends. Friends can disagree. But it's polite to figure out a conversation's mood before making comments, so you don't disrupt the discussion.

Let's Practice:

When another kid takes something you're using while you're playing, how should you react?

1. Tell the other kid you want it back — they probably didn't realize you were using it.
2. Scream and yell at the other kid and call them a thief.
3. Find a similar item for the other kid to play with as well.

The answer to this question is 1 and 3. Yelling and screaming and calling the kid a thief isn't a good strategy. Instead, calmly tell the other kid you want the item back, and offer to help them find something similar to play with.

Here's another scenario:

You get excited when you visit somewhere fun. Should you:

1. Match your level of excitement to everyone else in the room.
2. Establish a hand signal for your mom to use when she sees you need some calming down.
3. Continuously switch between activities without stopping.

4. Get people out of your way so you can take part in the fun activity.

The correct answers to this question again are 1 and 3. Watch everyone else in the room and match your level of excitement to theirs first. Then, when you get to the fun place, continuously change activities without stopping.

HANDLING REJECTION AND EXCLUSION

Everyone has been rejected or excluded at some point in their lives. Whenever this happens, it hurts a lot and can be hard to forget. Not everyone will be a good friend for you, so you'll need to decide when to keep trying, stand up for yourself, or when to just let go and move on. Below are some tips and options for handling rejection or exclusion. You can choose the ones that work for you in your particular situation.

Processing Your Feelings

It's okay to feel upset or hurt when you have been excluded from a group or activity. You should allow yourself to have those feelings and to express them.

You might want to wait to express those feelings until you are in a private place with people who make you feel safe and supported, rather than expressing those feelings in front of the people who made you feel rejected. Only share your personal feelings with those who you can trust to be kind.

Clarify What Happened

If you feel unfairly treated, such as being called out in a game when you did not believe you were out of bounds, consider that it might have been an honest mistake the first time it happens. If you continue being called out when you are not, then assume it was done on purpose. You should stand up for yourself and say, "I feel like I'm being called out when I'm not. Could we review the rules?"

Be Honest with Yourself

Ask yourself if you are doing or saying anything that might make other kids leave you out or not invite you. Do you do some things that might seem annoying to others? Do you sometimes sound bossy? Do you jump into the middle of games to mess them up on purpose? Ask your friends to give you an honest opinion about why others might be excluding you from activities.

Try Again

Just because you felt excluded from one group does not mean you cannot make friends. Every situation—and group of people—is different. So when you're ready, get back out there and meet new people. If you don't know anyone you can play with, you can ask a grown-up for help starting a game with other kids.

Let's Practice:

You ask a group of friends who are playing if you can join them. They say no. Should you:

1. Tell them you can wait to be a part of the next round.
2. Find other kids to play with.
3. Do the same thing to them in retaliation.
4. Mess up their game because they won't let you play.

Answers: 1 and 2

If they seem open to having you play their game but say there isn't any room, tell them you'd like to be part of the next round. If they don't seem to want you to play at all, find other kids to play with.

CHAPTER SEVEN:

INVITATIONS
WITH FRIENDS

Friends might spend lots of time together at school, clubs, or sports practice, and that's great. These are all good places to meet and enjoy spending time with your friends. But at some point you might want to do things with friends outside of those organized activities, like inviting them over to your house, or having your friend invite you over to their house.

In this chapter, we will refer to these visits as "playdates".

HOW TO BE A GOOD PLAYDATE GUEST

When you are invited to a playdate, it's helpful to know how to be a good guest. Using nice manners and making a good impression on your friend and their family will ensure they invite you back for more playdates in the future.

1. Arrive on time so your friend doesn't wonder if you're coming. Call your friend if you're going to be late.
2. Greet your friend and their parents politely. If they ask you to, take off your shoes when you go inside their house.
3. Decide with your friend what activities you want to do together. It's nice to offer to let your friend choose first.
4. Treat your friend's home and belongings with respect.
5. Ask before you touch or play with anything.
6. If you feel like you're getting bored or tired, try making suggestions for a different activity or game.
7. It's not okay to play with your friend's brother or sister and ignore your friend. Sometimes you

might all play together. That's great! But make sure your friend doesn't feel left out.

8. It's not okay to ask for snacks or open the refrigerator without permission.

9. It's not okay to snoop through drawers, closets, or cabinets, no matter what.

10. When your parent picks you up, you need to leave without getting upset. Politely say goodbye, and thank your friend for having you over. Let your friend know you will have them over to your house for a playdate soon.

Let's Practice:

You notice at a friend's house that they have many books you would love to read. Should you:

1. See if your friend would like to read together.
2. Tell your friend to watch TV while you read.
3. Take a book and go off to a quiet spot to read.
4. Ask your friend if you can borrow a book or two to read later.

Answers: 1 and 4

It's not polite to do one thing while your friend is doing something else. If you want to read, see if your friend wants to read with you, or ask them if you can borrow a book or two to read later.

Now that you know how to be a good playdate guest, let's talk about how to be a good playdate host.

HOW TO BE A GOOD PLAYDATE HOST

When you invite a friend over for a playdate, you should make sure they have fun and enjoy the playdate. These tips will help you successfully have a playdate at your house and make sure that your friend will be happy to come back again another time.

1. When your friend arrives, smile, say hello, introduce them to your parents and family members, and make sure they feel welcome.
2. Have some activities or games already planned to play with your friend. Ask them if they want to do those activities or play those games. You could create a puppet theater, play board games, make craft projects, or bake something together. It helps to make a list of ideas for activities or games and choose one from the list before your friend comes over.
3. Put away special things you don't want to share before your friend comes over.

4. Ask a parent to keep your brother or sister busy while you have your playdate, or find ways to include everyone in the playdate.
5. Offer your friends a snack and drink.
6. When you're the host, it's polite to do the activities your friend wants to do first.
7. It's also polite to let your friend go first when taking turns or sharing something when the playdate is at your house.
8. If the playdate isn't working out or is becoming boring, ask a parent to help you figure out what to do next.
9. Make sure you play with your friend — don't ignore them by reading a book, watching TV, or doing things alone.
10. When your friend is picked up, thank them for coming and walk them to the door. Don't start a new game while their parent is waiting. Let them know you look forward to the next playdate.

Let's Practice:

A friend wants to play something different than what you want to play. Should you:

1. Be sad and pout until your friend agrees to do what you want.

2. Tell your friend they're not your friend anymore.
3. Agree to take turns playing what each of you wants to play.
4. Decide what to play by using a choosing game, like flipping a coin or Rock, Paper, Scissors.

Answers: 3 and 4

When a friend wants to do something different than what you want to do, the best way to handle it is to either take turns doing what each of you wants to do or play a choosing game to choose what to do first.

Your friend starts to play with your favorite very special toy, and you don't want them to play with it. Should you:

1. Grab the toy away from them.
2. Tell them that the toy is special and to please be careful or nicely ask your friend to play with something else.
3. Scream at your friend to get their attention and yell at them that the toy is yours.
4. Be sure that all your special toys are put away and out of sight before you have a playdate.

Answers: 2 and 4

If you don't want your friend to play with your favorite toy, tell them the toy is special and nicely ask them to play with something else, or make sure all your special toys are out of sight before your playdate.

HANDLING DIFFERENT HOUSE RULES

You will find that there are different rules everywhere you go. Consider how library rules differ from those at football games. Some common activities like playing outside and watching TV may have different rules in your family and your friends' families, just to name a few. It will be necessary for you to adapt to different rules and make good decisions based on your own family's rules in different places and with different people.

1. You might have different rules in your family than others, and that's okay.
2. When you are at someone's house, you must follow their family's rules, even if you disagree with them.
3. You can respectfully say "No, thanks," or "My parents don't allow me to do that." If you are not sure, you can check with your parents.
4. If you have a friend over, you might want to remind them of the house rules. Make sure your friend feels welcome by using a friendly voice.

5. Hold your ground if your friend tries to get you to do something your family doesn't allow. "My parents and I have agreed on the rules, so I need to follow them," or just, "I don't like to break the rules," are good responses to use.
6. Say, "No, thanks," if your friend pressures you into breaking rules at your home or theirs.
7. The best thing you can do if you break a rule is to admit it and apologize. Your family or your friend's family will see that you are honest and responsible for your actions.
8. You should apologize to your friend's parents if you break the rules at their house.
9. Don't make a friend feel bad about their house rules being different from yours. Don't say things like, "I can't believe your mom won't let you do that." Every family has its own rules.

Let's Practice:

You are at your friend's house, and he is allowed to play M-rated video games but you are not. Should you:

1. Play the game with him but keep it a secret from your parents.
2. Suggest that you play a different game or do a different activity instead.
3. Tell your friend you have that game, even though it is a lie, so he won't make fun of you.

Answer: 2

A friend is over at your house and wants to sneak and watch videos on the Internet that you are not allowed to watch. Should you:

1. Tattle on him to your parents.
2. Tell him that you do not want to watch videos and choose another activity together.
3. Watch the videos so that he will not tease you or call you a chicken.
4. Nicely explain your house rule about videos and tell him that it is okay for him to watch them at his house later.

Answers: 2 and 4

PLAYDATE STRATEGIES AND ETIQUETTE

Playdates create and maintain real friendships. Here are some additional tips for successful playdates:

1. Maybe you are nervous about asking a new friend for a playdate. Even if you feel nervous, try asking them anyway. The worst thing that can happen is they say, "No, thank you." If that happens, say, "Okay, maybe another time." You might find that they really want to play with you later.

2. If you or your friend are very excited and running around, ask if they want to go outside.

3. If they say mean things about your family or other friends, tell them to stop.

4. Don't ditch your playdate for your friend's brother or sister, or for other kids who are around.

5. On a playdate, it's not okay to lie down or nap. You should always tell your friend, or their parent, that you are tired or unwell and you should reschedule the playdate.

6. Ask your friend to be gentle with your things if they are playing roughly with them.

7. On a playdate, remember that friendship is more important than being right.
8. When you and your friend cannot agree on what to do, be gracious and let your friend choose. You can also play a game like Rock, Paper, Scissors or flip a coin.
9. If you have problems or difficulties on a playdate that you cannot fix yourself, ask an adult to help you solve them.
10. Consider what went wrong and what you could have done differently if a playdate didn't go well. It always helps to talk to a grown-up about it.

Let's Practice:

You are having a playdate and you are getting tired. Should you:

1. Lie down on your bed to rest.
2. Suggest doing a quiet activity such as drawing or a board game.
3. Tell your friend you are tired, and they have to go home.

Answer: 2 or 3

If you have enough energy to continue the playdate, you could do a quiet activity. If your friend doesn't want to do that, or if you feel too tired to continue the playdate, tell your friend you're tired and they must go home.

You come home from a playdate and have a feeling it didn't go very well. Should you:

1. Forget about it, it's over.
2. Think about what went wrong and what you might have done differently.
3. Discuss your concerns with a grown-up.
4. Assume that your friend doesn't like you anymore and you will never be invited back.

Answers: 2 and 3

If you don't think the playdate went well, the best thing to do is to think about what went wrong and what you could have done differently. If you need help, you can discuss your concerns with a grown-up.

DECLING A PLAYDATE OR INVITATION TO PLAY

You may not be able to play if you are busy, or you might not feel that the person inviting you over is a good friendship match. You can politely decline a playdate invitation or leave the possibility open for another invitation.

1. You can say "no" to an invitation but do so without hurting the other person's feelings. Say, "No thanks, maybe later."

2. When someone invites you to play a board game, but you are busy or enjoying something else, you can say, "I'd like to play that game with you later, but right now I have to work on my building project." You could also say, "I would like to play with you, can you give me a couple of minutes to finish what I'm doing?"

3. Don't say, "No, I don't want to play with you," or "Go away, I'm busy."

4. If the game itself does not interest you, you could say, "I'd like to play with you, but I'm not a huge chess fan. Can we do something else together instead?"

5. If you are invited to a playdate or to a party and do not know if you can attend, say, "Thank you so much for inviting me. Let me see if I can go and then I'll get back to you."

6. If you haven't been able to play with someone who has asked you to play several times and you want to play with them, suggest another day that works for you.

7. Call your friend to reschedule a playdate if you can't go for any reason.
8. Tell your friend it's not a good time or that you need to check your family's schedule first if they ask to come to your house without your invitation.
9. It's okay to say that you've been very busy and aren't sure if your schedule will allow you to play but thank them for the invitation. They'll eventually ask other people for playdates instead of you.

Let's Practice:

Someone asks you to play, but you really don't want to. Should you:

1. Say, "No thanks, maybe later."
2. Tell them to go away.
3. Tell them that you don't like them and to leave you alone
4. Tell them that you don't feel like playing right now, and say, "But thanks for asking."

Answers: 1 and 4

These are the best ways to decline invitations to play with people who you really don't want to play with.

There is a kid at school who you have invited over for a playdate three times, who always says they are busy and they can't come. Should you:

1. Infer that the person is possibly not interested in a playdate and stop asking them.
2. Continue to ask that person every day about a playdate.
3. Tell them that the invitation is open and they can let you know if they ever want a playdate, and then start asking other people.

Answers: 1 and 3

This one is tricky. They may not be interested in playing with you. But if they are, the best way to handle it would be to tell them that the invitation is open and they can let you know if they want a playdate. Then start asking other people.

HOW TO WORK THINGS OUT AND SHARE

Making and keeping friends requires working things out and sharing. You'll often have to solve small problems before they become big ones, and you'll have to share items at home and at school. Let's start with how to work things out.

How to Work Things Out

1. You may have been told to "work things out" if you have a problem with someone. This is an important skill to have — if you don't try to work things out, your friends might get upset.

2. Grown-ups should remember that some kids don't know how to work things out yet and may need some extra help. If this happens to you, ask for help.

3. It can be hard to work things out. Most people prefer to have things their way all the time, but that's not possible.

4. Listen to the other person's point of view, opinion, or idea. Then politely explain why you disagree. Try to come up with a new idea or solution.

5. An example of how to work things out: You and your friend both want to be the red player in a game. You could say, "You want to be red, but so do I. How about we take turns being red, and flip a coin to see who goes first?"

6. You could also use a choosing game to decide something.

7. Checking game rules is often a good way to work things out. If the rules aren't in the game box, you can check them online.

8. It's sometimes a good idea to prioritize friendship over being right, going first, or winning the game. Occasionally, being more flexible than the other person is the right choice. But you need to stand up for your ideas and wants if a friend always wants their own way too.

9. Work things out using the three C's: Cooperate, Collaborate, and Compromise.

10. Whenever you get stuck on something, it might be time to agree to disagree, and come up with a new idea or game to play.

Let's Practice

You are out at recess. You want to play soccer, and your friend wants to swing on the swings. Should you:

1. Tell your friend they have to play soccer or you will not be their friend anymore.

2. Say, "How about we play soccer for half of recess and then go on the swings for the other half?"

3. Pick something else instead of soccer or swings that you can both agree on.

Answers: 2 and 3

In this case, playing soccer for half of recess and swinging on the swings for half of recess, or choosing a different activity you can both agree on would both be acceptable solutions this problem.

You and your friend disagree about what movie to watch. Should you:

1. Let your friend choose the movie this time and you choose the movie next time.
2. Ignore your friend's idea and put on the movie you want to watch.
3. Decide which movie to watch by flipping a coin.

Answers: 1 and 3

Letting your friend choose the movie this time and you choose next time or flipping a coin to choose which movie to watch would both be acceptable ways to choose a movie to watch.

SHARING

We all have to share with others often, even every day. It's not always easy to share things that we love—even for adults! But, as you know already, this is something you will have to do often in life. Sharing is very important in friendships, so be prepared to share with the people you care about. Refusing to share a toy or being greedy with a favorite snack might show a lack of care for your friends and hurt the trust between you. Here are some tips for sharing.

1. It's friendly to share before someone even asks.
2. When there is only one item available and many people want to use it, you might have to take turns. Using a timer to give each person an equal amount of time for their turn is a good way to do this.
3. Play Rock, Paper, Scissors or flip a coin to decide who goes first with a favorite item.
4. If you have to divide up something that everyone wants—like the last slice of pizza in the box—a good way to do this is by having one person cut the piece in half, and then the other person chooses which half they want. You could even be generous and offer your friend the larger piece.

Let's Practice:

You are riding a scooter and your friend wants to use it. Should you:

1. Say, "No! It's mine!"
2. Say, "I'm still using it, but you can use it when I'm finished."

94

3. Ignore your friend and keep riding.
4. Offer to take turns.

Answers: 2 and 4

These are the best answers because they give both you and your friend the opportunity to ride the scooter.

There is a big box of action figures at your after-school program and all the kids like to play with them. Should you:

1. Rush to get there after school and get all the action figures first.
2. Hide your favorite action figures where one else can find them.
3. Figure out how many action figures there are and divide them up between the kids who want to play with them.

Answer: 3

This is the best way to make sure all the kids who want to play with action figures can play with them.

CHAPTER EIGHT:

ACTIVITIES THAT HELP DEVELOP SOCIAL SKILLS

In this chapter, we'll discuss several games and activities you can use to build social skills and have fun at the same time. We'll discuss both interactive activities you can do and board games you can play.

INTERACTIVE ACTIVITIES

Staring Contest

You may have problems keeping eye contact during a conversation. Staring contests can help you practice maintaining eye contact so that you can focus on one task instead of communicating simultaneously.

If you feel uncomfortable, put a sticker on a friend or teacher's forehead and then start a conversation with them while looking at the sticker.

Virtual Playtime

What if you can't have a playdate in person? You can still video chat and hang out with your friends on the Internet. During video chats, you can look at your friend's screen to make eye contact.

Adaptability is an important trait, whether you are distancing yourself from other people or working in a new place in the future. Developing fun ways to spend time together improves problem-solving skills, which contribute to social skills.

Emotion Charades

This is just like regular charades, except you're describing different feelings using pieces of paper. Choose one from a bucket or hat, and then act it out.

This game helps you identify emotions based on body language and facial expressions. You can even adapt it into a game like Pictionary, where you have to draw a picture of the emotion.

Depicting and acting out feelings and reactions helps you learn how to manage your own emotions. This is important for forming positive relationships and communicating emotions to the people around you.

Expression Imitating Games

This game teaches you social skills through expressions. By imitating other people's expressions, you learn to recognize what they mean when others use them in real-life conversations.

When you understand facial expressions, you'll feel more confident when dealing with them.

Topic Game

Topic games have several variations, but the most popular one requires naming objects that relate to the topic that begin with each letter of the alphabet. In the case of animals, you may come up with:

- Aardvark
- Baboon
- Chicken

Etc.

Topic games teach you how to stay on one subject and follow directions until the activity is complete. You also learn to create connections and be creative with those letters that have fewer options.

IMPROVISATIONAL STORIES

Often, kids share stories even when they are not engaged in social skills activities. Improvisational stories require them to collaborate and create narratives without thinking ahead.

You can use cards or pictures that have words facing down for this activity. Using three of the cards, create a story that includes the topics or objects on each card. As soon as all the cards have been played, or once you've reached your story's end, the game ends.

This activity can be played as a game where everyone contributes to the development of one story and builds on each other's ideas. It can also be played as a solo storytelling activity.

NAME GAME

This easy game involves rolling or throwing a ball to a player after calling their name. This is a great social skills activity for learning classmates' names. Using someone's name shows that you care about other people and is a good way to get to know them better.

SIMON SAYS

When you play Simon Says, you develop discipline by being rewarded for following the rules. And you improve awareness, and impulse control by copying your classmates' movements and following instructions.

RHYTHM GAMES

Rhythm games are a great way to make music and learn how to follow directions and recognize patterns. Older kids could benefit from drumming — if you don't have a drum, you can use something like a laundry hamper placed upside down, or a pot and wooden spoon. While marching, tiptoeing, stomping, or hopping, you can drum different beats with your friends.

Another good rhythm game to play is Freeze. Play music and dance to it however you want. Then when the music stops, freeze in whatever position you're in until it starts again.

CHARACTER PLAY

With these social skills activities, you will be able to tap into your instinct to play. Use your stuffed animals to have conversations. This helps you practice social skills and can be a great way to show adults how you feel or to tell the story of something negative that happened to you, and not worry about hurting the toys' feelings.

TOKEN STACK

Board games such as checkers can be adapted to teach social skills such as how to have a respectful conversation. Each time you speak and respond appropriately, put another token on your stack.

Your challenge is to stack your tokens high while you take turns speaking. This helps you focus on maintaining a calm conversation and responding thoughtfully to questions and statements.

GAMES FOR MAKING DECISIONS

Playing decision-making games is a great way to develop social skills. Simple games and activities like matching and sorting teach persistence, thoughtfulness, and cooperation.

These games can help you with indecision because they teach you to decide, even if it's not the right choice at first. A mistake in these games will only have mild consequences, so you can just try again if you make a mistake.

Decision-making games include games like:

Musical chairs—Walk around a row of chairs while listening to music. Everyone must sit down in a chair when the music stops—if not, they are out. Continue removing one chair at a time until there is only one person left.

Tic-tac-toe — The classic X's and O's game. Make a grid of nine squares by making two horizontal parallel lines with two vertical parallel lines crossing through them. One kid chooses X, the other chooses O, and both players put their X or O in different squares until one person gets three in a row vertically, horizontally, or diagonally, or until there are no more squares left.

Ant or Elephant — Identify which animal you would prefer to be, using an ant picture or an elephant picture. Alternatively, you can choose between other animals, people, or qualities.

Hide and Seek — This is a classic game. One person hides while the seeker counts to ten (or another pre-determined number) and then starts looking for the person who hid. To make it more interesting, add a rule prohibiting hiding the same place twice. That means you'll constantly have to come up with new places to hide.

How the Story Goes — Have an adult start telling you a story, then at some point offer you two options. You get to choose how the story proceeds by choosing one of the paths they give you.

Pick Up Sticks — You can play this game with straws, skewers, or garden twigs. Your sticks should be upright on the table. Grasp the sticks and let them fall wherever they land. Pick up one stick at a time, removing it without moving any of the others.

Sticks lying on the surface and not touching others are easy, but those touching others need to be picked up carefully with your hands or another stick. Let the next player take a turn if you move another stick while trying to lift one.

At the end of the game, the player who has the greatest number of sticks wins. As you play, you will learn which sticks are lodged together too tightly to be moved easily and how moving one affects the others.

Memory — This game is played with several exact pairs of picture cards. All cards should be turned facedown on the table. You can take turns picking two cards and turning them face up. You keep the cards if they match. Flip them back facedown if they don't match. You should continue turning over two cards at a time until you have matched all cards. At the end of the game, the player with the most pairs of cards wins.

Building Game

When you build something with other children, like a tower with blocks, you have to communicate, take turns, and understand each other in order to bring your creation to life. Work with other kids to figure out how to build something. You'll learn how to try again if the project fails and celebrate each other's unique abilities when your project succeeds.

COMMUNITY GARDENING

Unlike other activities that teach social skills, community gardening teaches you how to care for plants as the living beings that they are.

When you garden with others, you learn responsibility because plants can't be neglected if they're going to live. This activity also allows you to get outdoors, which can be very calming.

Gardening can be difficult if you've never done it before. Some plants you can grow easily include:

- Snap peas—These sprout in ten days and mature in two months. You can eat them straight from the vine.

- Sunflowers—It takes a week for the seeds to germinate, and larger varieties will grow higher than you by the time summer is over.
- Radishes—These grow fast, you can harvest them after one month. It can be fun to see the little red globes popping out of the soil.
- Carrots—If you like to eat carrots, it can be fun to grow them. There is a longer growing season for them, so choose a smaller variety like Babette or Romeo.
- Potatoes—If you like potatoes, this can be another fun and easy one to grow. You can plant potatoes you buy at the grocery store, but you might have better luck with potatoes from a seed company.
- Green beans—Bush green beans grow fast and produce a lot. Due to their short height, they are quick to harvest. You'll also love hearing the snapping sound they make.

TEAM SPORTS

Team sports help you develop social skills and get some exercise at the same time. You can play sports at school, in a recreational league, or in the backyard with friends. As a team player, you'll learn how to work together to achieve a goal and stay focused throughout the game. During this process, you'll also learn to recognize emotional situations, such as when someone gets hurt or scores a goal, and respond appropriately no matter how you perform.

PRODUCTIVE DEBATE

Productive Debates work well to help you learn to manage your emotions and express yourself positively, even in difficult situations. As a result, you learn how to handle difficult conversations calmly without getting into an argument with the other person or insulting them.

By debating and listening to your opponents, you develop skills you will need in the classroom and in the workplace.

Possible debate topics could include:

- Should students go on field trips?
- Are outdoor classrooms helpful for learning?
- Are aliens real or fake?

- Should elementary school students learn advanced math?
- Should schools allow students to bring pets to class?
- Is homeschooling better than the regular educational system?
- Do students need recess?
- Should cell phones be allowed in the classroom?
- Does interactive learning have a place in the classroom?
- Will computers replace teachers in the future?

SCAVENGER HUNT

On a scavenger hunt, you work with other children so you can find objects or win prizes at the end of the activity. Scavenger hunts are a fun way to learn teamwork, organization, and positive decision-making skills. There are a lot of ways to reach the end of the game. You can split up, move as a group, and collaborate.

You are also rewarded for cooperating. These activities help you learn how to solve problems creatively when you create clues for others to solve.

Some scavenger hunt ideas include:

- Indoor scavenger hunt—Have a teacher or another grown-up make up a list of things for you to find in your house or school. It doesn't have to be specific items, it could be a general list, such as "something to read" or "something with buttons."

- Backyard insect scavenger hunt—Make a list of insects commonly found in a backyard. These could include flies, beetles, bees, ladybugs, and grasshoppers. Get a magnifying glass and see if you can find the insects.

- Sight word scavenger hunt—If you're learning sight words, go on a sight word scavenger hunt. Have a parent make a map of your house, or have your teacher make a map of your classroom. Write the letters from your sight words on paper, and cut them apart. Then have your teacher or parent tape them around your classroom or house in different places according to the map. Underline letters that could be mistaken if they were upside down, such as p and d and u and n. Once the letters are hidden in your house or classroom, it's time for the scavenger hunt.

- Sensory motor scavenger hunt—Make a list of things you can look for that involve the five senses. For example, something you can climb, something that is rough, something to play catch with, something that is soft, something that is loud, etc.

CHAPTER NINE:

HOW TO KEEP FRIENDSHIPS GROWING

By now, you should have a pretty good idea of how to make and keep friends, and some ideas of games and activities you can use to develop social skills. But what happens to your friendships as you get older?

As you get older, you or your friends' interests may change. You may spend less time together, and that's okay. You or your friend may even have to move if a parent gets a new job. How do you maintain your friendships despite all these changes? That's what we'll discuss in this last chapter.

TIPS FOR MAINTAINING FRIENDSHIPS

1. Remember what your friends bring into your life. Thinking about this will help you remember why you should keep trying.

2. Communicate in meaningful ways. There are a lot of ways to keep in touch with friends these days — email, social media, and even video chat. Whenever you are busy, it's tempting to reply to a message with an emoji — however, make sure to send a personal message. Consider sending a thoughtful email, or even better — a physical letter, a gift, or a phone call.

3. Make it a priority to spend time with your friends regularly. You can find the time, you just need to make a plan.

4. If you always seem to make plans and then break them, ask your friend when they want to do something. That should help you set and stick to a date.

5. Look at things from the other person's point of view. Say, "Let's meet up," and then suggest a movie with a certain actor you both love, or an activity you know you both will enjoy.
6. Decide what works best for you and your circumstances when it comes to seeing your friends. If you're involved in a lot of activities, you might not be able to see them as often.

Ways to Connect Across the Miles

What if you live far away and you can't see your friends as often as you'd like? Before the Internet, the only way you could see your friends was to physically go see them wherever they lived. Now there are a lot of ways you can connect with your friends, thanks to services like Netflix, Zoom, and different online gaming platforms. We'll talk through some of those options, as well as general tips for maintaining long-distance friendships.

BE COMMITTED

The most important factor in a long-distance friendship is the commitment of both friends to maintaining the relationship. So tell your friend how you feel! Make sure they know that their friendship is important to you and that you really want to work to keep it strong despite being far apart. If your friend feels the same way, then you're already off to a good start.

MAKE A PLAN

Talking together about how you are going to maintain this friendship from far away can help to make sure that it really happens. Have a conversation with your friend about the ways you want to communicate, and maybe even a schedule that might work for you both.

Do you and your friend prefer to send text messages to each other throughout the day, or to meet up for a video call twice per week? Do you like writing emails, or just talking on the phone? If you and your friend are on the same page about how you like to communicate and how often, that can help to make your friendship sustainable for the long run.

INVOLVE YOUR FAMILIES

If your parents and siblings know that this long-distance friendship is important to you and that you really want to work on maintaining it, then can provide you with support. Maybe they can make sure you're home on time for a weekly video call with your friend, or even help to plan for occasional visits to see your friend in person.

TOOLS AND SUGGESTIONS

There are so many great resources out there that help people to maintain relationships despite long distances. Here are some you might want to try out! Be sure to talk with your parents about all new apps or websites you want to try, and get permission before spending any money online.

A Streaming Party lets you watch TV shows or movies with your friends.

This Chrome extension lets you invite friends to watch a show or movie with you at the same time. Additionally, you can use the chat box to share commentary with each other during the episode.

Play Clue digitally.

You can buy Clue on the iOS app store and Google Play store and play it digitally with your friends. It has the same popular characters as the original board game, such as Mrs. Peacock and Colonel Mustard.

Use Co-Watching to look at memes on Instagram with friends.

If you like to video chat on Instagram, you can use co-watching to see what a video caller likes, bookmarks, and suggests on posts. The idea is to simulate the experience of scrolling through an app together.

Race your friends in Mario Kart Tour.

If you enjoy playing Mario Kart, you can download the mobile app and play the game with friends. You can download it from the iOS App Store and Google Play store. You can make additional purchases in the app, and you and your friends will need Nintendo accounts to play.

Play Monopoly.

Purchase the Monopoly game from the Google Play Store and iOS Store and download it to your mobile device to play it online with other players who also have the app.

Have a virtual gathering with Houseparty.

Houseparty lets you have a video chat with up to eight people. It's free to download on phones through the iOS or Google Play app stores. A few games are also available, including "Heads Up!" and trivia challenges.

Play a round of UNO! Online.

If you get tired of scrolling on social media, hanging out on Zoom, or doing the other things we've mentioned so far, play a round of online UNO! with your friends.

Play Wheel of Fortune online with your friends.

If you've ever watched this game show, now you can play it online with your friends in mobile versions, available on both Android and iOS platforms. You can download the game for free and make purchases in the app.

Get your friends together for a virtual trivia session with Kaboot!

This website is popular with teachers, but you can also use it to host virtual trivia sessions with friends and family. You can create free quizzes and send the links to as many people as you like.

Play Words with Friends if you enjoy word games

Users can have several Words with Friends games going at once, making it a great way to stay in touch with family and friends. You can download the classic version on the iOS and Google Play stores.

Play Games Online Through Your Computer

In addition to the apps mentioned above, you can play games on several websites with your friends who live in other cities or states. Among them are:

Gartic Phone

This is a web-based version of the Telephone Game. Make a room with some friends. The game can accommodate up to thirty players. You can play up to eleven different modes in this game, which combines drawing and sentence interpretation. Try writing silly prompts and copying your friends' funny drawings. You can find this game online, on the iOS App Store and Google Play Store.

Among Us

This game became very popular during the lockdown. It's a mystery game that's best not to play in person.

Work with a group of friends to complete several tasks to get your spaceship ready for the journey home, but be careful, as one of your crewmates is trying to sabotage your ship.

While they fix the ship, members are muted so they can remain anonymous—that's when the impostor kills a crew member. Crewmates win when they complete all the tasks or remove the impostor from the ship. If neither of those happens, the impostor wins.

Skribbl

If you enjoy being creative, this game is for you. It's basically an online version of Pictionary. Take turns drawing while the others guess what everyone is trying to draw. It's simple to use—just create a private room and share the link. Get as many points as you can because it's very satisfying to see your avatar win.

Board Game Arena

Play your favorite board games online with Board Game Arena. This website offers over 230 games, including a few of the games discussed in Chapter 8, like Catan, Cribbage, and Chess.

They also have other games available, such as Yahtzee, Bubble Pop, Jaipur, Marrakech, Bang, Rive, Duel, Lucky Numbers, and Solo.

Psych

If you're good at bluffing, get your friends together to play this game, which involves making up answers to trivia questions. The goal is to choose the correct answer from among all the incorrect ones.

Tabletopia

This is another website like Boardgame Arena. They have many different online versions of board games such as chess, checkers, and backgammon.

They also have card games like Texas Hold 'Em and Cards Playground, which consists of various card games, as well as many role-playing games, planning games, and number games like Lucky Number, which is a cross between a Sudoku puzzle and bingo.

In addition, you can use their editor to create new board games and even digital versions of paper games. You don't have to know any programming skills. You can also use their tools to test, demonstrate, and promote your games.

Colonist

This multiplayer online game is like Catan. You and your friends pretend to be settlers, building and developing settlements while trading and acquiring resources. When your settlements grow, you gain Victory Points.

The first player to reach a certain number of points wins. Creating a game room on the website is free and requires no download or registration—just set the room to private and share the link with three of your friends.

Risk

Play this online version of Hasbro's classic game as you deploy your troops and conquer territories. Play with AI, join or host online games with others, or invite up to five of your friends to join you. Plot to take over your friends' lands in this fun and intense game of strategy and planning.

Scrabble Go

If you're good with words, you'll enjoy Scrabble Go. With Scrabble Go, you can compete with your friends without being together in person. It's a free mobile game that plays just like the classic word game, but with additional features and game modes that make it even more fun.

With its colorful interface and simple controls, you can start a game at any time. Daily tournaments are a quick and instant way to play, but you can also play against your friends by inviting them or by logging in with your Facebook account. The objective of Scrabble Go is to score the most points, so get ready to grind out every word you know.

Codenames

This word-based party game requires at least four people. Two teams are formed — red and blue — with at least one guesser and one spy on each side. Guessers must select all their team's color words before the other team does first.

Be careful — black-colored words are also scattered throughout the board. These represent an assassin who will kill you if the guesser picks it. Since you can only communicate using one-word clues in this game, good communication with your friends is important. Creating a game room and inviting your friends is the best way to play — it's best to play with four to eight players.

Bunch

If you're still looking for different ways to play games with your friends on your mobile phone, check out Bunch. Bunch lets you play mobile games with your friends who live far away. It's similar to Discord, but tailored specifically for mobile games.

The app lets you and your friends host wholesome game night sessions on your mobile phone — simply connect to each other through a built-in video and audio chat system, then start a game together.

Their platform currently has six games that you can play with your friends. These games include Pool, an exciting racing game called Mars Dash, Draw Party, and the Flappy Bird multiplayer version. It also supports other games, such as Brawl Stars and Minecraft.

In addition, they've created relationships with other third-party game developers, which allow them to integrate other mobile games into the app. Some of the other games mentioned here, such as Risk, Scrabble Go, and Pysch, can also be played through Bunch.

CONCLUSION

I hope you've enjoyed this book and that it's given you some ideas and strategies for how to develop social skills, make new friends, and maintain your friendships over the years. As we finish up this book, take the time to answer these questions for yourself:

1. Which of the methods covered in this book do you think you'll use to start making friends with people?

2. If you already have a few good friendships, what will you do to continue to nurture those friendships over the years?

3. What strategies could you use to keep in touch with your friends when you eventually move away from one another?

There are no right or wrong answers to these questions—they're simply meant to help you think about how you can use the information provided in this book to make new friends and continue developing the friendships you already have. Good luck to you as you continue expanding your circle of friends!